EMMANUEL JOSEPH

The Health of Nations, Political, Psychological, and Business Insights into Global Well-Being

Copyright © 2025 by Emmanuel Joseph

All rights reserved. No part of this publication may be reproduced, stored or transmitted in any form or by any means, electronic, mechanical, photocopying, recording, scanning, or otherwise without written permission from the publisher. It is illegal to copy this book, post it to a website, or distribute it by any other means without permission.

First edition

This book was professionally typeset on Reedsy.
Find out more at reedsy.com

Contents

1   Chapter 1: The Intersection of Politics and Health   1
2   Chapter 2: Psychological Factors in National Health   3
3   Chapter 3: Economic Influences on Health   5
4   Chapter 4: The Role of Business in Health   7
5   Chapter 5: The Impact of Globalization on Health   9
6   Chapter 6: Health Systems and Policy   11
7   Chapter 7: Health Equity and Social Justice   13
8   Chapter 8: The Role of Technology in Health   15
9   Chapter 9: Health Communication and Education   17
10   Chapter 10: Environmental Health and Sustainability   19
11   Chapter 11: Global Health Governance   21
12   Chapter 12: Health Ethics and Human Rights   23
13   Chapter 13: Health and Education   25
14   Chapter 14: Cultural Determinants of Health   27
15   Chapter 15: Health and Global Development   29
16   Chapter 16: Future Directions in Global Health   31
17   Chapter 17: Conclusion: Building a Healthier Future   33

1

Chapter 1: The Intersection of Politics and Health

Politics and health are deeply intertwined, with policies and governance greatly affecting national and global well-being. Political stability, for instance, has a direct impact on healthcare infrastructure, access to essential services, and overall public health outcomes. Effective health policies foster environments where citizens can thrive, while political turmoil often leads to health disparities and challenges in delivering care. Understanding this intersection allows us to appreciate the critical role political frameworks play in shaping health outcomes across populations.

Furthermore, the allocation of resources and prioritization of health initiatives are inherently political decisions. Governments influence the direction of healthcare spending, the development of health technologies, and the implementation of preventive measures. Political ideologies also shape attitudes toward public health, determining whether health is viewed as a collective responsibility or an individual burden. As such, political leadership and vision can either bolster or hinder health advancements, making the study of political systems essential to comprehending health dynamics.

International relations and global health diplomacy further underscore the connection between politics and health. Collaborations between nations through treaties and global health organizations facilitate the sharing of knowledge, technology, and resources. These partnerships aim to address transnational health challenges such as pandemics, climate change, and infectious diseases. Therefore, the health of nations is not solely a domestic matter but is influenced by the global political landscape, necessitating a holistic approach to political and health strategies.

Finally, political activism and advocacy play crucial roles in promoting health equity and justice. Grassroots movements and civil society organizations often push for reforms that prioritize marginalized and vulnerable populations. Political engagement by citizens can lead to policy changes that address social determinants of health, such as education, housing, and employment. Understanding the power dynamics at play in the political arena empowers individuals and communities to demand and achieve better health outcomes for all.

2

Chapter 2: Psychological Factors in National Health

The psychological well-being of a population is a key component of national health, influencing both individual and collective health outcomes. Mental health, in particular, has gained recognition as a crucial area of public health, with its impact spanning across various aspects of life. High levels of psychological distress can lead to increased rates of chronic illnesses, substance abuse, and suicide. Therefore, addressing mental health is essential for achieving holistic health and well-being.

Psychological factors such as stress, anxiety, and depression can have profound effects on physical health. Chronic stress, for instance, is associated with an increased risk of cardiovascular diseases, weakened immune function, and metabolic disorders. It is important to recognize the bidirectional relationship between mental and physical health, where one influences the other. National health strategies must prioritize mental health services and interventions to improve overall health outcomes.

Social determinants of mental health, such as socioeconomic status, education, and social support, also play a significant role in shaping psychological well-being. Individuals from disadvantaged backgrounds are more likely to experience adverse mental health outcomes due to factors like financial strain, lack of access to quality education, and social isolation. Addressing these determinants requires comprehensive policies that promote social equity and create supportive environments for mental health.

Furthermore, cultural attitudes and stigmas surrounding mental health can hinder individuals from seeking help and receiving appropriate care. Stigmatization of mental illness often leads to discrimination, social exclusion, and reluctance to access mental health services. Public health campaigns and educational initiatives are essential to changing societal perceptions of mental health, encouraging open discussions, and reducing the stigma associated with mental illnesses.

3

Chapter 3: Economic Influences on Health

Economic factors are significant determinants of health, influencing access to resources, healthcare services, and overall quality of life. Wealth disparities within and between nations contribute to health inequities, with poorer populations experiencing higher rates of illness and mortality. Economic stability and growth are therefore essential for improving health outcomes and reducing health disparities.

Income levels directly affect individuals' ability to afford healthcare, nutritious food, and safe living conditions. Higher income is generally associated with better health outcomes, while lower income correlates with increased exposure to health risks and limited access to care. Economic policies that address income inequality and provide social safety nets are crucial for promoting health equity and ensuring that all individuals have the opportunity to achieve good health.

The role of employment and working conditions in health cannot be overlooked. Job security, fair wages, and safe work environments contribute to physical and mental well-being. Conversely, unemployment, underemployment, and hazardous working conditions can lead to stress, injury, and poor health. Policies that promote decent work and protect workers' rights are vital for creating healthy societies and improving public health.

Additionally, the economic burden of healthcare on individuals and families can have long-lasting effects on health and financial stability. High out-ofpocket healthcare costs can lead to delayed care, financial hardship, and medical debt. Universal health coverage and affordable healthcare systems are essential for reducing the financial barriers to care and ensuring that everyone has access to the services they need without experiencing financial strain.

4

Chapter 4: The Role of Business in Health

The business sector plays a pivotal role in shaping health outcomes through its influence on employment, innovation, and corporate responsibility. Businesses have the power to create healthy work environments, promote employee well-being, and contribute to the broader community's health. Corporate policies that prioritize health and wellness can lead to improved productivity, reduced absenteeism, and enhanced overall well-being.

Innovation in the business sector drives advancements in healthcare technologies, pharmaceuticals, and medical devices. Research and development investments by businesses lead to the creation of new treatments, diagnostic tools, and health solutions. Partnerships between businesses, governments, and academic institutions are essential for fostering innovation and ensuring that new health technologies are accessible and affordable.

Corporate social responsibility (CSR) initiatives also contribute to public health by addressing social and environmental determinants of health. Businesses can support community health programs, promote sustainable practices, and reduce their environmental impact. CSR efforts that focus on health equity and sustainability can lead to positive health outcomes and strengthen the relationship between businesses and communities.

Furthermore, the marketing and consumption of products by businesses can significantly impact health. Companies have a responsibility to market products ethically and promote healthy choices. The food and beverage industry, for instance, plays a critical role in shaping dietary habits and influencing nutrition-related health outcomes. Responsible marketing practices and the availability of healthy options are essential for promoting public health and preventing chronic diseases.

5

Chapter 5: The Impact of Globalization on Health

Globalization has profound effects on health, creating both opportunities and challenges for global well-being. Increased interconnectedness and the flow of goods, services, and information have led to significant health advancements, but they have also contributed to the spread of diseases and health disparities. Understanding the impact of globalization on health is crucial for developing effective strategies to address global health challenges.

One of the positive aspects of globalization is the sharing of medical knowledge and technologies across borders. Collaborative research and international partnerships have led to breakthroughs in medical treatments and public health interventions. Global health organizations and initiatives, such as the World Health Organization (WHO) and the Global Fund, play essential roles in coordinating efforts to combat diseases and improve health outcomes worldwide.

However, globalization also facilitates the rapid spread of infectious diseases, as evidenced by pandemics like COVID-19. Increased travel and trade create pathways for pathogens to cross borders, requiring robust global health surveillance and response systems. International cooperation and coordination are essential for preventing and managing infectious disease outbreaks, ensuring that countries are prepared to respond to health emergencies.

Economic globalization has both positive and negative impacts on health. While increased trade and investment can lead to economic growth and improved health outcomes, they can also exacerbate health disparities. Developing countries often face challenges in accessing essential medicines and health technologies due to patent protections and trade agreements. Ensuring equitable access to health resources requires addressing the complexities of the global economic system.

Globalization also influences lifestyle and behavioral health factors. The spread of Western dietary patterns and sedentary lifestyles has contributed to the rise of non-communicable diseases (NCDs) such as obesity, diabetes, and cardiovascular diseases. Public health strategies must adapt to the changing global context by promoting healthy behaviors and addressing the social determinants of NCDs.

6

Chapter 6: Health Systems and Policy

The structure and functioning of health systems are critical determinants of population health. Effective health systems provide accessible, quality care to all individuals, regardless of their socioeconomic status. Health policy decisions shape the design, financing, and delivery of healthcare services, influencing health outcomes and health equity.

Universal health coverage (UHC) is a key goal for health systems, ensuring that all individuals have access to essential health services without financial hardship. Achieving UHC requires comprehensive health policies that address financing, service delivery, and workforce development. Countries with strong health systems prioritize primary care, preventive services, and equitable access to care, leading to better health outcomes.

Health system performance is influenced by governance, leadership, and accountability mechanisms. Transparent and accountable health governance ensures that resources are used efficiently, services are delivered effectively, and populations' needs are met. Strong leadership in health systems is essential for setting strategic directions, implementing policies, and responding to emerging health challenges.

Health systems must also be resilient to withstand shocks and adapt to changing health needs. Resilient health systems can maintain essential services during crises, such as pandemics or natural disasters, and quickly recover from disruptions. Building resilience requires investments in infrastructure, workforce, and technology, as well as fostering collaboration across sectors.

Integration of health services and intersectoral collaboration are important for addressing the social determinants of health. Health systems must work with other sectors, such as education, housing, and social services, to create supportive environments for health. Coordinated efforts can lead to comprehensive care that addresses the root causes of health disparities and promotes overall well-being.

7

Chapter 7: Health Equity and Social Justice

Health equity and social justice involve addressing structural and systemic factors that contribute to health disparities. This includes tackling issues such as discrimination, poverty, and unequal access to education and healthcare. Policies and interventions aimed at promoting health equity must consider the social, economic, and environmental contexts that influence health outcomes. By addressing the root causes of health disparities, we can create a more just and equitable society where everyone has the opportunity to live a healthy life.

Community engagement and empowerment are essential components of health equity and social justice. Involving communities in the decision-making process ensures that health policies and programs are responsive to their needs and priorities. Grassroots movements and community-based organizations play a crucial role in advocating for health equity and holding policymakers accountable. Building partnerships with communities fosters trust and collaboration, leading to more effective and sustainable health interventions.

Moreover, health equity and social justice require a focus on vulnerable and marginalized populations. These groups often face multiple barriers to accessing healthcare and achieving good health, including stigma, discrimination, and lack of resources. Targeted interventions that address the specific needs of these populations are necessary to reduce health disparities and promote social inclusion. By prioritizing the health and well-being of marginalized groups, we can move closer to achieving health equity for all.

8

Chapter 8: The Role of Technology in Health

Technology has revolutionized the field of health, providing new tools and solutions for improving health outcomes and delivering care. From electronic health records (EHRs) to telemedicine and wearable devices, technological advancements have transformed how we prevent, diagnose, and treat illnesses. The integration of technology into healthcare systems has the potential to enhance efficiency, accessibility, and quality of care.

Telemedicine, for instance, has expanded access to healthcare services, particularly for individuals in remote or underserved areas. Through virtual consultations, patients can receive medical advice, prescriptions, and follow-up care without the need for in-person visits. Telemedicine also facilitates continuity of care and reduces the burden on healthcare facilities, making it a valuable tool for addressing healthcare disparities and improving patient outcomes.

Wearable devices and health monitoring technologies enable individuals to track their health metrics in real time, such as heart rate, physical activity, and sleep patterns. These devices empower individuals to take an active role in managing their health and making informed lifestyle choices. Additionally, health data collected from wearables can be used to identify trends and inform public health interventions, contributing to population health management.

The use of artificial intelligence (AI) and machine learning in healthcare has opened new possibilities for diagnostics, treatment planning, and personalized medicine. AI algorithms can analyze large datasets to identify patterns and predict health risks, enabling early intervention and preventive care. Machine learning models can also assist in clinical decision-making by providing evidence-based recommendations and supporting healthcare professionals in delivering precise and effective care.

9

Chapter 9: Health Communication and Education

Effective health communication and education are critical for promoting health literacy and empowering individuals to make informed health decisions. Health communication encompasses a wide range of activities, including public health campaigns, patient-provider interactions, and health information dissemination through various media channels. Clear and accurate communication is essential for conveying health messages and encouraging positive health behaviors.

Public health campaigns play a vital role in raising awareness about health issues and promoting preventive measures. These campaigns use various strategies, such as social marketing, mass media, and community outreach, to reach diverse audiences and convey health messages. Successful campaigns are tailored to the target population's cultural and linguistic needs, ensuring that health information is accessible and relevant.

Patient-provider communication is a cornerstone of effective healthcare delivery. Open and empathetic communication between healthcare professionals and patients fosters trust, enhances patient satisfaction, and improves health outcomes. Health professionals must be skilled in communicating complex medical information in a way that patients can understand and act upon. Additionally, involving patients in shared decision-making empowers them to take an active role in their care and make choices aligned with their values and preferences.

Health education initiatives aim to improve health literacy and provide individuals with the knowledge and skills needed to manage their health. Health literacy involves the ability to access, understand, and use health information to make informed decisions. Educational programs in schools, workplaces, and communities can enhance health literacy and promote lifelong health behaviors. By investing in health education, we can create a more informed and health-conscious society.

10

Chapter 10: Environmental Health and Sustainability

The health of nations is closely linked to the health of the environment. Environmental factors, such as air quality, water quality, and climate change, have significant impacts on public health. Addressing environmental health issues and promoting sustainability are essential for protecting and improving population health.

Air pollution is a major environmental health concern, contributing to respiratory and cardiovascular diseases, as well as premature mortality. Reducing air pollution requires policies and interventions that target the sources of pollution, such as industrial emissions, transportation, and energy production. Promoting clean energy and sustainable transportation can mitigate air pollution and improve health outcomes.

Water quality is another critical aspect of environmental health. Access to safe and clean water is fundamental to preventing waterborne diseases and ensuring overall well-being. Efforts to protect water sources, improve sanitation, and manage wastewater are essential for maintaining water quality and safeguarding public health. Additionally, addressing issues such as chemical contamination and harmful algal blooms is crucial for protecting water resources.

Climate change poses significant threats to global health, including heat-related illnesses, vector-borne diseases, and food and water insecurity. Mitigating climate change requires a comprehensive approach that includes reducing greenhouse gas emissions, promoting renewable energy, and enhancing climate resilience. Public health strategies must also include adaptation measures to protect vulnerable populations from the health impacts of climate change.

Sustainability practices, such as reducing waste, conserving natural resources, and promoting biodiversity, contribute to environmental health and well-being. Sustainable development goals (SDGs) provide a framework for integrating environmental, social, and economic considerations into health policies and practices. By prioritizing sustainability, we can create healthier environments and ensure the well-being of current and future generations.

11

Chapter 11: Global Health Governance

Global health governance involves the coordination of international efforts to address health challenges and promote global well-being. International organizations, such as the World Health Organization (WHO), play a central role in setting health standards, providing technical assistance, and facilitating collaboration among nations. Effective global health governance is essential for addressing transnational health issues and achieving health equity.

The WHO, established in 1948, is the leading international health authority responsible for guiding and coordinating global health efforts. The organization sets global health standards, monitors health trends, and provides technical support to countries in addressing health challenges. The WHO also plays a crucial role in responding to health emergencies, such as pandemics, by coordinating international responses and providing guidance to affected countries.

Global health governance also involves partnerships between governments, non-governmental organizations (NGOs), and the private sector. These partnerships leverage the strengths and resources of different stakeholders to address complex health issues. Collaboration among diverse actors is essential for developing innovative solutions, sharing best practices, and ensuring that health interventions reach those in need.

International treaties and agreements, such as the International Health

Regulations (IHR), provide a legal framework for global health governance. The IHR, adopted by the WHO member states in 2005, aim to prevent and respond to public health risks that have the potential to cross borders. The regulations establish procedures for reporting and managing health emergencies, ensuring that countries are prepared to address global health threats.

12

Chapter 12: Health Ethics and Human Rights

Health ethics and human rights are fundamental principles that guide the practice of public health and healthcare. Ethical considerations in health involve issues such as autonomy, beneficence, non-maleficence, and justice. Ensuring that health policies and practices are ethical and respect human rights is essential for promoting health and well-being.

Autonomy refers to individuals' right to make informed decisions about their health and healthcare. Respecting autonomy requires providing individuals with accurate information, obtaining informed consent, and respecting their choices. Healthcare professionals must balance the principle of autonomy with the need to protect public health, particularly in situations where individuals' decisions may impact others.

Beneficence and non-maleficence are ethical principles that emphasize the importance of doing good and avoiding harm. Healthcare professionals have a duty to act in the best interests of their patients, providing care that benefits them while minimizing potential harms. Ethical dilemmas may arise when the benefits and risks of interventions are uncertain or when resource constraints limit the ability to provide optimal care.

Justice in health ethics involves ensuring that health resources and opportunities are distributed fairly and equitably. Health disparities based on factors such as race, gender, socioeconomic status, and geography must be addressed to achieve health equity. Policies and interventions should prioritize vulnerable populations and work towards eliminating systemic barriers to health.

Human rights in health encompass the right to the highest attainable standard of health, as recognized in international human rights treaties. This includes access to healthcare, essential medicines, and the underlying determinants of health, such as food, water, and shelter. Protecting and promoting health as a human right requires a commitment to social justice and the empowerment of individuals and communities.

13

Chapter 13: Health and Education

The relationship between health and education is bidirectional, with education influencing health outcomes and health impacting educational attainment. Access to quality education is a social determinant of health that shapes individuals' opportunities and well-being throughout their lives. Promoting education is essential for improving health and achieving health equity.

Education has a profound impact on health by influencing health behaviors, knowledge, and decision-making. Individuals with higher levels of education are more likely to engage in healthy behaviors, such as exercising regularly, avoiding tobacco use, and seeking preventive care. Education also enhances individuals' ability to understand and use health information, enabling them to make informed health decisions.

Health, in turn, affects educational attainment and academic performance. Children who are healthy and well-nourished are more likely to attend school regularly, perform better academically, and complete their education. Conversely, health issues such as chronic illnesses, malnutrition, and mental health disorders can hinder educational progress and limit opportunities for future prospects. Health issues can lead to absenteeism, decreased concentration, and lower academic performance, creating a cycle of disadvantage that perpetuates health and educational inequities. Ensuring that students have access to healthcare services, proper nutrition, and mental health support is crucial for their academic success and long-term well-being.

Moreover, schools play a critical role in health promotion by providing health education and fostering healthy environments. Comprehensive health education programs equip students with the knowledge and skills needed to make healthy choices and adopt lifelong health behaviors. Schools can also implement policies and practices that promote physical activity, healthy eating, and mental well-being, creating a supportive environment for student health.

The relationship between health and education extends beyond the individual level to impact communities and societies. A well-educated population is better equipped to address public health challenges, engage in health-promoting behaviors, and advocate for health equity. Investments in education yield long-term benefits for population health and economic development, creating a positive feedback loop that enhances overall well-being.

14

Chapter 14: Cultural Determinants of Health

Culture plays a significant role in shaping health beliefs, behaviors, and outcomes. Cultural factors influence how individuals perceive health and illness, seek care, and adhere to treatment. Understanding the cultural determinants of health is essential for delivering culturally competent care and promoting health equity.

Health beliefs and practices vary widely across cultures, reflecting diverse worldviews and traditions. Cultural beliefs about the causes of illness, appropriate treatments, and the roles of healthcare providers can impact health behaviors and decision-making. For example, some cultures may emphasize holistic approaches to health, while others prioritize biomedical interventions. Healthcare professionals must be culturally aware and respectful of these beliefs to provide effective care.

Language and communication are critical components of cultural competence in healthcare. Language barriers can hinder access to care, lead to misunderstandings, and affect treatment adherence. Providing interpreter services, culturally relevant health information, and linguistically appropriate care are essential for improving communication and health outcomes for diverse populations.

Social norms and cultural practices also influence health behaviors, such as dietary habits, physical activity, and health-seeking behaviors. Public health interventions must consider cultural contexts to be effective. For example, health promotion campaigns should be tailored to resonate with the target population's cultural values and practices. Engaging community leaders and cultural brokers can enhance the acceptance and impact of health interventions.

15

Chapter 15: Health and Global Development

Health is a critical component of global development, influencing economic growth, social stability, and human capital. Investments in health contribute to poverty reduction, economic productivity, and sustainable development. Recognizing the interconnectedness of health and development is essential for achieving global well-being.

Healthy populations are more productive and capable of contributing to economic growth. Good health enables individuals to work, learn, and participate in societal activities, fostering economic development. Conversely, poor health can hinder economic progress by reducing labor productivity, increasing healthcare costs, and limiting opportunities for individuals and communities.

Global development initiatives, such as the Sustainable Development Goals (SDGs), prioritize health as a key driver of development. The SDGs emphasize the importance of achieving universal health coverage, reducing health disparities, and addressing the social determinants of health. Integrating health into development policies and programs ensures that health is a central consideration in efforts to achieve sustainable development.

Health and development are also interconnected through the concept of human capital. Human capital refers to the skills, knowledge, and health of individuals, which contribute to their ability to participate in and contribute to society. Investments in health and education enhance human capital, leading to improved economic and social outcomes. By prioritizing health as a fundamental aspect of development, we can create more equitable and prosperous societies.

16

Chapter 16: Future Directions in Global Health

The future of global health is shaped by emerging trends, challenges, and opportunities. Advancements in science and technology, shifting demographics, and changing disease patterns will influence global health priorities and strategies. Preparing for the future requires adaptive and forward-thinking approaches to address evolving health needs.

One of the key trends shaping global health is the rise of non-communicable diseases (NCDs). As populations age and lifestyles change, NCDs such as cardiovascular diseases, diabetes, and cancer are becoming leading causes of morbidity and mortality. Addressing the growing burden of NCDs requires comprehensive strategies that include prevention, early detection, and management. Promoting healthy lifestyles, reducing risk factors, and improving access to care are essential components of NCD prevention and control.

Technological advancements will continue to drive innovations in healthcare delivery and public health. The use of digital health technologies, such as telemedicine, electronic health records, and mobile health applications, will expand access to care and improve health outcomes. Artificial intelligence and machine learning will play increasingly important roles in diagnostics, treatment planning, and personalized medicine. Leveraging these technologies requires addressing challenges related to data privacy, equity, and ethical considerations.

Global health will also be influenced by environmental and social determinants of health. Climate change, urbanization, and migration present both challenges and opportunities for public health. Addressing the health impacts of environmental changes and promoting sustainable development are critical for protecting population health. Additionally, social determinants such as education, housing, and economic stability will continue to shape health outcomes and health equity.

Furthermore, global health governance will need to adapt to emerging health threats and changing geopolitical landscapes. Strengthening international cooperation, enhancing health systems' resilience, and ensuring equitable access to health resources are essential for addressing global health challenges. Building on the lessons learned from past health crises, such as the COVID-19 pandemic, will inform future strategies for health preparedness and response.

17

Chapter 17: Conclusion: Building a Healthier Future

The health of nations is a multifaceted and dynamic concept, influenced by political, psychological, economic, and cultural factors. Achieving global well-being requires a holistic and integrated approach that addresses the complex interplay of these determinants. By prioritizing health equity, investing in health systems, and promoting sustainable development, we can build a healthier and more equitable future for all.

Political leadership and governance play a crucial role in shaping health outcomes. Effective health policies, equitable resource allocation, and international collaboration are essential for addressing health challenges and promoting global health. Advocacy and activism are also important for holding policymakers accountable and ensuring that health remains a priority on the political agenda.

Psychological well-being is a fundamental aspect of health that must be addressed through comprehensive mental health services and supportive environments. Reducing stigma, promoting mental health literacy, and integrating mental health into primary care are key strategies for improving psychological well-being. Recognizing the impact of social determinants on mental health is essential for addressing the root causes of psychological distress and promoting holistic health.

Economic factors influence health by shaping access to resources, healthcare services, and opportunities for well-being. Reducing income inequality, promoting decent work, and ensuring affordable healthcare are vital for achieving health equity. Economic policies that prioritize health and well-being can lead to improved health outcomes and contribute to sustainable development.

Cultural competence and respect for diverse health beliefs and practices are essential for delivering effective and equitable care. Health systems must be responsive to the cultural contexts of the populations they serve, ensuring that health services are accessible, relevant, and acceptable. Engaging communities and fostering cultural understanding are important for promoting health equity and improving health outcomes.

In conclusion, building a healthier future requires a collective effort to address the complex and interconnected determinants of health. By fostering collaboration, investing in health systems, and promoting equity and justice, we can create a world where everyone has the opportunity to achieve their full health potential. The health of nations is a shared responsibility, and together, we can work towards a future of global well-being.

The Health of Nations: Political, Psychological, and Business Insights into Global Well-Being

In this comprehensive exploration of global health, we delve into the intricate web of factors that shape the well-being of nations. The book examines how politics, psychology, and business influence health outcomes, providing a holistic understanding of the multifaceted nature of health.

We start by exploring the intersection of politics and health, highlighting how governance and political stability impact healthcare systems and public health. We then move into the realm of psychological well-being, discussing the profound effects of mental health on overall health and the importance of addressing psychological factors.

Economic influences are also a key focus, as we analyze how wealth disparities and economic policies shape access to healthcare and quality of life. The role of businesses in health is explored, emphasizing the impact of corporate practices, innovation, and social responsibility on public health.

Globalization's impact on health, the structure of health systems, and the importance of health equity and social justice are examined in detail. We also discuss the critical role of technology, effective health communication, environmental health, and global health governance.

As we look to the future, the book highlights emerging trends, challenges, and opportunities in global health. By addressing these complex and interconnected determinants of health, we aim to build a healthier, more equitable future for all.

www.ingramcontent.com/pod-product-compliance
Lightning Source LLC
LaVergne TN
LVHW020459080526
838202LV00057B/6037